Computer Programming Language: The Blueprint

Learn the Basics of Computer Programming Languages

By: Cyber Punk Architects

Disclaimer Notice:

Please note the information contained within this document is for educational and entertainment purposes only. Every attempt has been made to provide accurate, up to date and reliable complete information. No warranties of any kind are expressed or implied. Readers acknowledge that the author is not engaging in the rendering of legal, financial, medical or professional advice.

By reading this document, the reader agrees that under no circumstances are we responsible for any losses, direct or indirect, which are incurred as a result of the use of information contained within this document, including, but not limited to, — errors, omissions, or inaccuracies.

About CyberPunk Architects

Computer programming doesn't have to be complicated. When you start with the basics its actually quite simple. That is what Cyberpunk Architects are all about. We take pride in giving people the *blueprint* for everything related to computer programming and computer programming languages. We include Python programming, Raspberry Pi, SQL, Java, HTML and a lot more.

We take a sophisticated approach and teach you everything you need to know from the ground up. Starting with a strong base is the only way you will truly master the art of computer programming. We understand that it can be challenging to find the right way to learn the often complex field of programming especially for those who are not tech savvy. Our team at Cyberpunk Architects is dedicated to helping you achieve your goals when it comes to computer programming.

We are here to provide you with the *blueprint* to give you a strong foundation so you can build on that and go into any area of programming that you wish. Our architects are comprised of professionals who have been in the industry of information technology for decades and have a passion for teaching and helping others especially through our books. They are friendly, experienced, knowledgeable computer programmers who love sharing their vast knowledge with anyone who has an interest in it.

We look forward to getting a chance to work with you soon. Here at Cyberpunk Architects, you can always be sure that you are working with right people. Allow us take care of your needs for learning computer programming. If you have any questions about the services that we are providing, please do not hesitate to get in touch with us right away.

Check out all of our books at:

Bit.ly/Cyberpunkbooks

As a THANK YOU for purchasing our books we

want to give you **a free bonus**. **A quick guide on how to get started with programming**. This book covers the basics of what you want to know to get started.

Free Bonus!

Programing can be hard but it doesn't have to be! Take this free PDF guide to understand some of the basics of programming

Download the free guide:

bit.ly/cpfreeguide

Table Of Contents

Introduction

Working in coding can be a great thing to learn. It allows you to learn more about how your own computer works and can be a fantastic way to keep it safe and make some of your own programs. Too many people assume that computers and the programming that goes with them are just going to be too hard for them to learn without them having years of experience or school, but the reality is, anyone is able to learn a coding language, you just need to pick one and get started.

This guidebook is a great resource to help you to get started with some of the most popular coding languages that are in use right now. We will start out with some of the basics of computer programming and why you would want to learn one of these languages, before moving on to the basics of starting with this one and how to make it work for your needs. Some of these are great all on their own, and some will be better when you combine them with another coding language to get even better results.

Inside this guidebook, we are going to learn some of the best coding languages, some of the most popular, which will help you to get started on the right track. Inside we are going to look at some of the basics, and how to write your first codes, for some of the most popular coding languages including C#, C++, Python, Java, and JavaScript. With these basic coding languages you will be able to work on almost any of the coding languages that you would like including making your own websites and other programs.

When you are ready to learn a bit more about some of the best coding languages out there and you want to get started on your own, make sure to check out this guidebook and see how easy it can be to get started on some of the best coding languages from above.

Chapter 1: Why Learn About Computer Programming

Computer programming is a great skill to learn how to use. Most people are worried that computer programming is going to be too hard for them to learn. They feel that unless they spend a lot of time learning the computer or having to spend years at school in order to do anything. But even as a beginner, it is easy to learn how to work with computer coding. In the following chapters, we are going to talk about some of the basic coding languages that are really popular and will help you to learn how to get started and you will be able to see how easy computer programming can be.

You don't have to do something that is too complicated when you are getting started. You won't have to know how to hack onto some of the other computer systems or create operating systems or anything like that when you are first getting started. If you want to get to that later on, it is something that you can work with, but for now, some of the basics are all that you need to get started and have a good time. Let's take a look at some of the reasons that you would want to learn how to work on computer programming before we move on to some of the best coding languages that you can use to get the most out of your new coding skills.

Make your own programs

One of the best options that you can do when it comes to using a new coding language is that you are able to make some of your own codes. Each of the coding languages will have their own options when it comes to what you are able to create. For example, C# is a more advanced option that can handle some of the bigger projects that you want to work on while Python is good for those who are beginners and Java and JavaScript are great for when you want to work on your own websites and the add-ons that come with them.

You will find that there are so many programs that you are able to make when it comes to a coding language and you are able to design almost anything that you would like.

One good idea to work with is to make sure that you figure out what kinds of projects that you would like to work on and then figure out what coding language that you would like to work on to make that project a reality. The only limitation is your imagination when it comes to the things that you are able to create.

Answer questions when things go wrong

No matter what kind of computer you have, there are always times when something will go wrong. The computer could run into an issue with a new program that you are working on or it may get a virus or another issues. Sometimes the computer gets old and just needs a little bit of extra help compared to some of the others.

When these things go wrong, many times we are going to try to find a computer professional and pay them a lot of money in order to get them all fixed up. We get the problem fixed in this manner usually, but we have no idea of the type of issue that was going on or even how it was fixed in the first place. This is fine for some people, but wouldn't it be nice if we were able to understand what is going on with our computers and even how to fix them ourselves?

When you learn a bit about coding, you may be able to fix some of the issues on your own. You will be able to use some of the coding to take a look through the issue that is coming up on your screen and make some changes. You maybe will be able to figure out that the new program you installed is not the best one for your particular computer program, perhaps you placed something in the wrong order, or you can make some simple changes.

The coding that you will learn may not be able to fix all of the issues that come up, but you will find that it can make a bit difference in how well you can take care of and fix the issues on your computer.

Learn more about computers

Even if you don't have any ideas for programs in mind right now, it is still a great idea to work with a new coding language. You are going to be surprised by how much it is able to teach you about your own computer.

These coding languages are going to help you to manipulate and change around the things that are going on in your computer, whether you are trying to look things up or to make a new program. In this guidebook, many of the programs that we are going to do concentrate on the Hello World program to get started, so that you can get used to them and you get to see how your computer will react to each of the codes.

Many times we are going to get into a new coding language and be uncertain about what we are doing. Most of us have not spent the last many years working in computers and making them our own. But with the help of a new coding language and learning something new, we will learn so much great stuff about how our computers work.

Chapter 2: The C# Programming Language

The first language we are going to work with is the C# programming language. This is a very popular coding language, but it is considered an intermediate one to learn. You will like that there is a lot of power that comes with this coding language and it is very easy to learn how to use and create your programs from. To get started with some of these options, make sure to visit this website to download the C# language: http://www.microsoft.com/en-us/download/details.aspx?id=7029

What are the variables?

When we bring up the topic of variables in our code, we are talking about the names that we give to all the data that is inside our programs; these data types are ones that we want to store for now but which we may want to manipulate a bit later on. For example, if you want to store the age of your user inside of the program, you would need to name the data, using the userAge, and then declare that this is a variable userAge with the following statement:

int userAge:

This declaration statement will be used in order to state the data type that is going with the variable and then the name as well as the data type will refer to any data that is stored inside of the variable (which depending on the code can be either some text or a string of numbers). Since we used the variable (int) for this example, the code is going to show that there will be an integer inside, which is something that works since we want to get an age, or a number. After you take the time to declare the variable of userAge, the program will save some space in the memory of your computer so that this data can be stored. You can come back and find this variable later on and access any of the data, even making some modifications, simply by using the right name later on.

The data you will see inside of C#

When it comes to picking out the data types, there are some variety that comes with this kind of language. Some of these we are going to talk about throughout the book because they are common and will work on many of the codes that we are trying to write. Some of the most common data types that are found in this language include:

Int: this is the one that will stand for integer. It is going to be a number of some sort, as long as it doesn't have a decimal or a fraction in it.
Char: this is the one that will stand for character. It is a single unit inside of the code and it can be used in order to store that single character. You can add together characters inside the code to get what you would like.
Bool: this one is going to stand for Boolean and it is based off the idea of being either true or false. It is often used to help out with control flow statements and will check to see whether your answer is true or false based on the conditions that you are using.
String: this is the one that is used any time that you would like to create, manipulate, or even compare different pieces of text that are inside of the code.

Another data type that you will probably utilize a lot when working in C# includes the operator. These operators are really busy in the code because they are responsible for doing so many